Autumnal Glimpses

Lynn Radford

BookLeaf Publishing

Presentation by *BookLeaf Publishing*

Web: www.bookleafpub.com

E-mail: info@bookleafpub.com

ISBN: 9789357617499

First edition 2022

To the world I love and all the souls I share it with, both animal and human; I am a product of my environment which has been ripe for the taking in this season of my life. I am deeply grateful for all of the relationships and experiences that inform my work.

ACKNOWLEDGEMENT

Writing is a solitary endeavor undertaken by the bravest among us. It happens when the words inside us can be contained no longer. Sometimes it is enough to pour the words onto paper. Other times, it feels as though the very words themselves urge the writer to go further still.

To all writers, whether your words are ever read, or are read with loving care, I applaud your bravery and tenacity!

To all of the family and friends who put up with us when we are consumed with words, Thank You!

PREFACE

Autumn is a second spring when every leaf is a flower. ~ Albert Camus

Fall is this author's favorite season. My love of fall stems from my earliest memories of leaves on pavement from my stroller as a child. As I wrote, I experienced those memories once again, while sharing them with the inspiration of the current season.

Ode to a Kite

As you fly overhead,

your colors splayed in midair,

I find myself freed

by the tranquility of the moment.

When the wind dies down, you falter

and slowly descend your perch.

Chains of reality invade my peace,

bringing me to Earth as well.

Summer is Over

Sun-warmed breezes of summer

replaced by cool, icy air —

No boats float down the river.

No kites fly overhead.

Everyone is grounded.

It'll be winter by and by.

Just now summer is over —

It drifted past us quickly

like clouds up in the sky.

Gone

The bright summer sun,
Gone in the blink of an eye!
When next the sun rose,
T'was a winter sun again.
Devoid of the warmth promised.

Autumn Vibe

Orange —

Brown —

Gold —

Red!

Leaf Peeping.

Crisp —

Clear —

Cool —

Fall!

Passing quickly.

Sweaters —

Blankets —

Boots —

Cozy!

Snuggling in.

The Power of Time

Silence.

Another cacophony

Energies thrummmm —

Pulsating openly.

Golden.

Illumination

Quiet's soft glow

Dawning the new day.

Age.

—Out of time?

— Aquarius?

Ancient questions, both.

Old.

Over-the-hill —

Not long for this world —

Vintage Antiques.

First Day of School

New clothes! New shoes!

First Day of School!

The Emperor's got nothin' on me!

I'm feelin' fine!

I'm on cloud nine!

I like what I see in the mirror!

Here comes the bus!

I'm in a rush!

I didn't see the puddle!

Covered in mud,

my spirits plunge.

There goes my big debut!

What happened next?

My friends, they laughed

And clapped me on the back.

"Those kicks are rad!"

"I saw your shirt in the store."

"What a way to break them in!"

And they all laughed some more!

Appearances

Crayola crayons
And freshly sharpened pencils
Mead Trapper Keeper
All ready for the Big Day!
I'm not ready — for fifth grade

Football Season

Pep Rallys

Cheerleaders

Marching Bands

Footballs

Shoulderpads

And Helmets

August thru December

And sometimes beyond

Weekends

Turf Green

And Bright Lights

Quarterbacks

Touchdowns

Cheering Crowds

GO TEAM, GO!

Hunter's Moon

Rise! O' Hunter's Moon!
Arcing brightly overhead
Golden orb of light
Her zenith reached whilst I slept
Her moonbeams guiding my dreams

Majestic Maple

Majestic Maple
sun's rays dance upon her leaves
Red luminary
A glowing beacon of fall
Grand Duchess of all the trees

The Nut Man

Long before you see him,
The unmistakable scent
of cinnamon roasted nuts
tells your nose he's there.

You'll find him without fail
that first Saturday in October,
tucked amongst carmel apples
kettle corn and apple cider.

Warm pecans and almonds
coated in a crispy glaze
of sugared cinnamon spice
await watering mouths.

Autumn Leaves

Rake at the ready
He gathers wisps of color
Soon, there'll be a pile

Autumn Chimes

Chimes ring in warning
in the shadows of the leaves
touched by autumn air
and left swinging in the breeze.
Not just music in their wake.

The Coyotes

The howls were terrifying,
I felt naked and alone.
A brick house stood between us
still, the sound did chill my blood.

A cry that wasn't howling
echoed with tremendous fear —
I knew then, they'd been hunting.
That the creature's end was near.

My husband grabbed a flashlight.
"You can't go out there!" I cried.
It was then he grabbed his gun
and stepped into the night.

Eyes glowed low in the light's beam
and their howls did stop at once.
Immediately, they ran!
And they haven't been seen since.

Late Fall

Overnight the view has changed
from one of golden splendor
to one that's far more bleak —

Barren branches stretch and reach
for leaves that blew away —

There they'll stand, through winter, frozen.
Waiting until spring.

The Ghost

She drifts along the falls
Empty and alone she sails
No one can hear her silent calls
None can hear her desperate wails.

She is bound to roam alone
Existing on no earthly plane
Trapped in realm all of her own
She sings her sad, mute refrain.

Some have felt her presence here
As she reaches for the 'ever after'
But none will ever know her fear
To never again hear laughter.

The Halloween Party

Halloween party
Decked out in black and orange
Spooky costumed guests
Eating creepy-themed goodies
Dancing to the Monster Mash

Haunted House

Creaking, Moaning,
Long dark halls,
Stale breathy sighs —

Flames gutter,
Webs shudder,
Shadows deepen in the night —

Eyes see,
Ears hear,
That which cannot be spoken —

Chill envelops
Frazzled nerves
Nothing left to calm them —

Creeping 'round
Ev'ry curve
The panic is consuming!

Halloween

Leaves are falling
on the ground —
Little goblins
all around —

Scary pumpkins,
Candlelight,
Ghosts and goblins —
What a fright!

Trick or Treat
is what they say
Hoarding candy
for another day.

Memories

Not present, nor future
　　　　but past —

An image, a song
A scent, a voice —

Mere months ago,
Yesterday, or yesteryear —

Childhood —

Relationships —

Adventures —

Life's key moments
　　　unlocked —

Sad? Joyful?
Bittersweet?

The stuff of dreams
and nightmares —

Fall's Final Frost

Glist'ning, frost-kissed leaves
Tender blossoms bow their heads
Autumn days slip by
Winter's edging closer still
As the leaves fall from the trees

www.ingramcontent.com/pod-product-compliance
Lightning Source LLC
Chambersburg PA
CBHW062205160726
48282CB00027B/999
9789357617499